To -

A K...

gone to Adaho!

MW00638935

THE
MOCKINGBIRD
POEMS

R.B. MORRIS

Published by

RICH MOUNTAIN BOUND
Books
Music
Woodwork
Photography
Sculpture

www.richmountainbound.com
www.rbmorris.com

Mockingbird Illustrations by Karly Stribling

Book Design by Aaron Russell

A Library of Congress Cataloging-in-Publication
Case Number:1-989100363

ISBN 978-0-615-86211-8

Other works by the author

Poetry

Keeping the Bees Employed
Early Fires

Music

Rich Mountain Bound
Spies Lies and Burning Eyes
Empire
Zeke and the Wheel
Take That Ride
Knoxville Sessions
Local Man

Drama

The Man Who Lives Here Is Loony
A one-man play
based on the life and work
of James Agee

To the backyard

The Mockingbird Poems

The
Mockingbird
Poems

Genesis

In the beginning was the Word
And then there was Mockingbird

In the beginning was the Lie
And a shadow flew over

In the beginning was the Sound
Haunting the unborn air

And it was the air
And it was the unborn

Waiting for harmony
Waiting for Mockingbird

God's Sound Check

When God was setting it all up
The way it is
Mockingbird was there fluttering
Around between
His ears

When God plugged it in
All the fear and trembling
All the love and murder
All the crashing waves
And synchronicities
All the calibrations
And determinations
How hot a kiss
How loud a stink
How sick a taste
How long a tooth
And how it would look
To the emergent beasts
All the while He was tweaking
The secret frequencies of a tweet
Of light whistling around
In that endless night
Nodding out divine vibrations
And golden echoes to the mix

He knew all this swirling
Of the ethers and clumping
Of the clay into further
Convergences would amplify
His myriad transformations
And produce some graven
Good sounds

Cool, thought God, dialing in
A last ravel of constellations
This is good
Let them touch everything
And burn if they burn
Or learn if they learn
And let's get this symphony cooking

Mockingbird in the Garden

Mockingbird played with his mate
They sang in the holly trees
And ate when they were hungry
Mockingbird held a red berry in his beak
He said, my darling, this red berry
Is like the evening sun we sing to
Like your lovely eye unblinking in air
I would give it to you
But there are so many, get your own
And without another word
Mockingbird ate the berry
And began a song

Mockingbird in Winter

When the hard rains fell
Mockingbird huddled up in the trees
He was full of moths and
Really didn't care
He had sung late the night before
Perched upon a corner pole
With only an old drunk to hear
The water poured off Mockingbird's beak
His feathers fluffed and his bones chilled
As the thunder rolled and the rains fell
Mockingbird thought about putting stones
In his mouth and singing

Mockingbird's Vocation

When Mockingbird was sick he had no doctor
When he was depressed there was no therapist
When he needed enlightenment there was nothing
When he was broke and he always was
What difference did it make?
Mockingbird had no recourse but to sing

Mockingbird in the Olden Wooden Days

In the days of wine and roses
Mockingbird held court

He was entertaining on the verandas
And rock gardens where

The lost generation lounged
When the barbarians arrived

Mockingbird rode herd above them
Beckoning apocalypse

Trumpeting it all along
In the morning when everyone

Had a headache Mockingbird was
Nowhere to be found

But by midday when a few jays
Had begun to cut up

There he was in a low tree
Dealing the deck

By the time of the flood
Mockingbird declared himself

First mate and slept in the crow's
Nest as he pleased

When they finally hit land
Mockingbird flew off

And made a few quick deals
With the natives

A great emissary, Mockingbird
He spoke their tongue

And sang their song
We love you, he said

Later when they asked him
To be king, Mockingbird said

1- Okay
2- No thanks, I have work

3- Sure, but I don't do requests
4- Be our king! Be our king! Be our king!

Mockingbird and the Crows

Monkey see monkey do, said Mockingbird
Monkey see monkey do, he said
But there were no monkeys around
Only a murder of crows off
To the side of the road
Monkey see monkey do, said Mockingbird
And the trailing crow shot back one
Shiny black eye and cursed
Cawing and falling in line
Monkey see monkey do, said Mockingbird
One more time

A Cawcophony of Crows

Can he talk, said Crow
Can he even talk?
I think not, said Crow
I think not
I think not, said another Crow
I think not, said another
Then in the next tree over
He can't tawwk
He can't tawwk
I think nawwt
I think nawwt

The young crows didn't get Mockingbird
What's his deal, they wanted to know
What's he crowing about sitting
Up in our tree stealing our songs?
Old Crow just ruffled his feathers
Sniffed the air mumbled the weather
Looked to the highway dumpster
Then out to the fields where
Turkey buzzards were circling
Answer enough, he felt
Don't make me say it
The word comes down but
I don't always have to bring it
These boys will learn
They'll see soon enough
Talk amongst yourselves, he said
And flapped back to the rear

The wagon train was beginning to roll
I'll cruise to the far field, he thought
Hook up with the boys

Have a little toast
A little grub of the old feast
Leave the bones and swing on
To the parade
Caww the rear flank!
Caww the all clear! he dreamed

But when he touched down
There was old Mockingbird
Already railing his shtick of Crow
And wailing a woeful lament
Opening up the evening air
Reaching to the firmament
Son of a bitch, said Crow
That old haint has stormed
The stage and planted a flag
Listen at him slammin' that rag
What a drag, he intoned
What a bag of shit
And I was so looking forward to this
He sighed the high weary sigh
Of an old linguistics master
And avoided the eyes
Of his vaunted colleagues
Ah well, he concluded for all
Shall we sail us to a distant wood
Lest this Bo weevil sidetrack
The whole progression
It's all good, said Crow to his bro's
But his day was ruined

Mockingbird and the Native Americans

Mockingbird fell for a Robin
She seemed such an exotic bird
His mouth moved in unexpected ways
And it had been days since he had sung for anyone
This Robin was so young and curious
And such a beautiful breast
Mockingbird would love to rub his beak
Through her feathers and be close to her colors
What is your genealogy, said Mockingbird
Have I seen you before?
I am a red breast, said Robin shyly
And native to the Great South
My eggs go back unto these hills
They say I have a dove's mouth
Mockingbird just hummed
And continually adjusted his wings
He began to sing like Robin and would often
Bring her a worm in the evenings
Is this just a seasonal thing, thought Mockingbird
And soon she'll go off with her own kind?
It was true, one day without a word
Robin was gone
And Mockingbird was left
To sing his own song

Mockingbird and the Political Ramifications

Mockingbird was keeping rough company
Negotiating a small arrangement
Okay, he said, I'll strike up the band
At your command
Just so long as you leave this dirt alone
Bluejay was pacing slyly
Focused on distant trees
He didn't say a thing
He snatched a worm
From between his feet
That was my worm, said Mockingbird
I'm trying to think, said Bluejay
I can understand that might
Take time, sighed Mockingbird
Trying not to chime
Okay, said Bluejay, it's a deal
I'll be sucking eggs when the eagle flies
And a little bird can kiss it goodbye

All I have to do is conjure up a tune
While some sparrow goes down
For a drink, said Mockingbird
And as long as my beak is as long
As the creek and all that's heard is a song
I get to keep all the worms
That are already mine
Now is that so wrong?

Portrait of the Young Bard As Mockingbird

Yeah sure, said Mockingbird
I remember Whitman
When he was just a boy
Nights on the beach
I would sing and he would
Space out
A great listener that kid
That's when I first
Started singing and flying
At the same time
And he'd run along with me
A little game we played
Had a funny way he'd run
Like he was about
To light down
On the sand
And then he would
And not move a muscle
So long as I kept singing
Flutin' out ore the waves
Yeah, those were great days
Said Mockingbird
He gave me some of
My first big reviews
The attention being on me
And not the Sea
Said he, the spoken bird

The Assassination of Mockingbird

Mockingbird got arrested once
But he wouldn't talk

The big guy said, you gonna
Sing for us little bird?

Mockingbird wouldn't say a word
How would you like your wings

Clipped? they asked him
Or maybe we trim that beak for you?

Mockingbird was mum
After they tortured him

Mockingbird said, that's okay
Today is a good day to die

He had heard that before
So they put Mockingbird in a vice

And squeezed the life out of him
Then they left him dead

On a lonely street
No one suspected a thing

God Made a Hillbilly

When God handed out the endless attributes
On the ladder of love and go get it
He gave some the ability to fly
Of those He gave some the ability to sing
Of those He gave some dominion
Over the air and earth
Of those He made Mockingbird

In my image I have reckoned, said God
I reckon so, said Mockingbird

Yodeling His Way to the Big City

T for Texas
T for Tennessee, sang Mockingbird
M for Mississippi
M for me, sang he the dusty troubadour
I am the king billy of all these high
Lonesome hills, declared Mockingbird
This is my sovereign domain
This sky, these trees, this hill
I am the deal, sang the king of sing
I am what it's about
I'm about as slick as it gets, he mused
I'm the cat's meow
I'm the sleeping dog's dream
He howled
Let me tell you
I'm the song of the South
I'm a scenic highway, he rolled on
I'm a rural route
I'm bending this note, sang the maestro
I'm putting it down
I'm coming around, he allowed
I'm moving up town
Yeah, said Mockingbird
I'm moving uptown

The Muse Arrives

Mockingbird stared through the glare
Of the city bus windows
He felt a cloud wiggle behind him
He watched a woman walking three dogs
A kid on a bicycle wearing a blindfold
He saw the dopey swans swell
Across the city pond
A beer truck rolled up its side door
And a car horn alarm kicked on
The hot midday sun
Tied it all in a blaring knot
Mockingbird, who couldn't blink
Loosened the ropes
Cleared his throat
And began to sing

Mockingbird and Billy Blake
Rambling 'Cross the Cityscape

Mockingbird couldn't help it
He wrote a new song
Someone interrupted and there
He went again
I'll see you up on Gay Street, he sang
They're swinging down on Vine
We'll all hook up on Depot
And catch the crosstown line
We'll hop that city bus, he crooned
With a paper and a cork
We'll hum the noonday rush
Harmonize the news and sports
I'll shoot you through the hoops, he tolled
Cause you can't get there straight
I'll drop you at the palace
You can pay me at the gate

Mockingbird Connects with the Underground

Mockingbird read NOTES FROM UNDERGROUND
This Dostoevsky is a strange worm, he thought
He ought to get out more
Maybe climb a tree
Mockingbird began a letter to Dostoevsky
An aria mail soliloquy
Pushing the envelope with a ripple of possibilities
Arise and fly! sang the god of air and sky
Come out and join your brother in crime!

Mockingbird Carlos Mockingbirds

everything
depends upon

me
said mockingbird

in the green tree above
the red truck while

two black dogs played
in the yellow field

Mimus and the Polyglottos

When Mockingbird first heard rock
He cocked his head and crapped
What in hell is that?
It sounded like a train wreck
Someone was screaming
Someone's banging on garbage cans
Mockingbird swooped down
Between the chains of the porch swing
And swung by the backdoor and
Out the other side causing the cat
To jump and knock over a flower pot
He stopped dead still in a Carolina pine
As a guitar solo sailed over the
Rumbling clang of a fast moving
Train through a Georgia night
It was raining but it wasn't raining
Mockingbird couldn't figure it out
Some kind of train?
Some kind of big tractor?
A hurricane or flood?
Some kind of disaster was happening
Mockingbird turned his x-ray sonar radar
On the garage door that hung ajar
There were people in there
All yelling and jumping around
Like they was walking on hot coals
Of fire, said Mockingbird
He was reminded of the holy rollers
Handling their big worms
On Sunday mornings
But this was different
This was bigger
This was Saturday night

And it was so loud the moon
Stuck his head in a cloud
Mockingbird couldn't hear his
Voice for the noise
But he hung around
He was spellbound
Something in the sound
Was speaking to him
His blood pounded and rolled
To the mighty locomotion

Mockingbird stayed until the final crash
Until they packed it in and drove away
They've left the building, said Mockingbird

Mockingbird didn't go home that night
He flew downtown
He found some friends
They raved about the sound
Word got around
Others had heard
They started making that sound
They started layin' it down
The news got out
There's good rockin' tonight
And if that Mockingbird won't sing
I know a bird that can do that thing
Sang Mockingbird
He and his mates got with it
They were working the late shift
Bouncing sounds off every wall
All the poles and corner signs
Manhole covers and warehouse doors
The courthouse bell the city clock
They were rockin' round the block

It was intoxicating work
Yeah Mockingbird was singing the blues
But he was loving it too

The usual birds were all shook up
Reviews were in the pit
But old MB was having a ball
Mixing it up with the mighty chiefs
He swore he'd never quit
High O Silver! sang Mockingbird
Yeah Yeah Yeah
I can't stop loving you, he said
I can't slow down
I can't help myself, he went on
I'm Cathy's clown
I'm all tore up
I'm all tore down
It's her town now, said Mockingbird
Let's get out of this place

Mockingbird and his mates
Blew out the city gates
They flew the coop
They busted out
For the high and wide
For the high and lonesome
And every low place between
Like a wheel on fire
Just him, a few chickadees
And the boys
And all for the love
Of that joyful noise

Mockingbird as an American Outlaw

Mockingbird got too high
He was mocking things before
He heard them
And he heard everything
That was his strength and his weakness
In his strength, said Mockingbird
He had heard that
Help me in my weakness, he remembered too
Oh yes, Mockingbird was a joker and a thief
A drifter and a lonesome hobo
A poor immigrant and a barefoot servant too
And he dreamed three kings and St. Augustine
And down along the curb two riders
Were obstructing his telegram to Tom Paine
But Mockingbird felt so good
He just sailed away

Mockingbird and the Sun

First thing in the morning
The sun was shining
And Mockingbird was climbing the scale
Is this Gloria? said Mockingbird
Is what Gloria?
I think thus I am, said Mockingbird
I link thus I yam
Thus I yam not spam, say it he
I am what I am and I pan what I can
It was a perfectly clear day
You couldn't find the edge between
The bright orb and the blue garb
Somebody somewhere is doing some
Important work, said Mockingbird
Some work where important body, said bird said
As he flew through a fluster of gnats
And a crewcut cat rubbed a high shoulder
Through honeysuckle
Scat! said Mockingbird
Cut throat cur! said yakking sir the bloke
I'm choking on morons, say it!
Here, take a note to Seymour Krim
Tell him the juice is in
And I'm jumping on a hot street
Dear Sy, do you dig Bobby Bly?
He's gonna make a man
If he don't get outta hand
I be diggin Bobby Blue Bland, said Mockingbird
I be diggin the long worm in the dark sand
Bobby White, Bobby White, said bird said bird
I be diggin Bird!
100% White!
I be diggin Bird!

Mockingbird and the Journalists

Mockingbird was interviewed for a magazine
Apparently it was something everybody read
He was feeling at ease in that open book kind
Of way and rather philosophical for that time
Of morning

I eat bugs, said Mockingbird
I eat bugs, slugs, grubs, gnats, moths
Flies, butterflies
Anything that flutters by, said Mockingbird
And berries
And cherries, yes cherries
When I can get them
And worms, of course
I avoid feeders, said Mockingbird
Not my style

The photographer was in constant
Motion circling and angling Mockingbird
Snapping countless shots
Mockingbird eyeballed him
But was focused on the interviewer
Who appeared somewhat serious
Somewhat intrigued

So, what is this thing with bugs?
He wanted to follow up

I vanquish bugs with a magic wand
Also known as my beak
Said Mockingbird
I crush and swallow them
I extinguish their existence

To sustain my own, he said
Mockingbird paused so
The interviewer could
Get it all down

I know I am no better
Than the bug,, Mockingbird continued
I am no better than the bug
He repeated

The interviewer looked up
You feel okay about that? he casually
Queried with overtones abounding

Look, said Mockingbird who
Could see where it was going
I am the tiger that eats your children
The lightning that burns your house
I move things along, okay?
Arumpa pum dumb
Arumpa pum dumb, said dodo the bird
I'm the big wind that blows you down
I'm just saying, said Mockingbird
But so it goes, he went on
So it goes
What would you propose?
Said Mockingbird
What would you propose?

Well, it would be nice to keep my house
Said the interviewer
It all sounds so brutal
But would you say you add to
Or take away? he reasonably quipped

Every day, said Mockingbird
Every day
It's a brutal poodle
It's a rigged pig
A deranged arrangement
It's heaven sent
It's a cruel jewel
It's sane and insane
It's plain and un-plain, said Mockingbird
It's yin and yang
It's bing and bang, baby
It's all there
Every day, said Mockingbird
Every day

So, life is really just so much give and take?
A balanced enough question, he felt
Confident in his symmetry

Yes and no, said Mockingbird
No and yes
It's a cycle
It's a season
It's sparks from a chimney, said Mockingbird
It's a mating call
It's a feeding frenzy
It's the big crunch
It's the fishes and loaves
It's the naked lunch
It's a dirge
It's a funeral train, he chugged
It's Tarzan in the jungle
It's you in the shower
It's all a song, said Mockingbird
It's all a song

41

It sings itself
We sing along
Sometimes it helps, said Mockingbird
Come on
Come on, he said
It's a chorus
It runs right through us
Can't you hear it?
It comes around
Like the moon, said Mockingbird
Like the moon that moves the tides, he said
Like the moon that moves the tides
Like the moon that moves the tides
He said one more time
And I start to sing
I take a ride
I find a tree
Some tattered wire
It doesn't matter
Anywhere
And I light my fire, said Mockingbird
I light my fire

But does it last? the one with the pen
Boldly asked. *Your fire?*
Does it stand the test of time?

The test of time? said Mockingbird
The test of time?
Time Time Time, said Mockingbird
What Time?
Do you believe in Time, said Mockingbird
Is that the name of your magazine?
He had begun to sing
Do you believe in Space?

Is that the name of this place?

The name of what place? the interviewer asked
They were sitting in Centennial Park

Where you are, said Mockingbird
Where you are
What do you call it? You call it what?

Oh, we don't call it anything
The interviewer answered
We just ask questions for our readers

For our readers, said Mockingbird
For our readers, our readers
Where are they? asked Mockingbird
Are they in Time?
Are they in Space?
Is there time to have space?
Is there space to have time?
We all die, said Mockingbird
We all die
Even I, said Mockingbird
Even I
The song doesn't end
The song doesn't end, he said again
It comes to me
Again and again, said Mockingbird
Again and again
We all die
Again and again, he said he said
Again and again
We all die
Even I, said Mockingbird
Even I
But we all live, he said

We all live
Even you, said Mockingbird
Even you

The interviewer was still writing
When Mockingbird flew into
A cloud and disappeared

The Arts Council According To Mockingbird

Mockingbird was trying to work with the city
When they cut down his house
He compromised and kept singing
When they asked that he move again
He said, okay I'll work it out
When they brought the interstate over his head
He said, you know this is going to effect my music
When they tunneled beneath his tree
Mockingbird began to wonder if the city
Really appreciated what he was doing
It's not like I'm getting
Rich over this, said Mockingbird
It's not like I'm making
A salary like the rest of you guys
It just so happens I like my work
Is that so wrong?
Mockingbird got very disheartened
He said, the city doesn't understand artists

Mockingbird and the People

Mockingbird was puzzled with people
He sat astride a road sign
And studied them from a distance
Mockingbird tilted his head and looked closer
He shivered at what he saw and shook it off
He stropped his beak on either side
Of the sign and peeked again

What is this Man? asked Mockingbird
What does he do?
He has no wings and rides in machines
He moves in herds and shoves into boxes
He squawks an ugly talk and staggers about
Like he was walking in mud
Like he lost his eyes
His head is shaped like a hairy egg
And never hatches into anything
And I'll be a son of a bitch
If he can carry a tune in a bucket
Said Mockingbird

What kind of artist can he be?
Asked the prince of melody
He tries to hold things rather
Than let them fly
You can't put the wind in a jar!
Bellowed the one whose voice
Moves clouds

He has no beak! He blew on
He can hardly speak much less sing!
He has to go inside and
Wail his woe into a box

So he can turn the knobs
And make it spin
Just to hear it again
Then mock himself
Squawking back at it
Til he's drunk and falls over asleep
Dizzy old hairy old egghead, he said
What kind of artist
Can he be?
Can he be?
Can he be?

God and Mockingbird Talking

You were gone before you were here
Said God
And you'll be gone again

Gone before I was here
Gone again, said Mockingbird
What does that mean?

That means you're here forever, said God
Don't worry about it
You're here

I don't get it, said Mockingbird

I don't get it, said God

I don't get it, said Mockingbird

You're part of forever, said God
Just go with that and see where
It takes you

Just go with that, said Mockingbird
Just go with that
Okay, said Mockingbird
I'm going with that
I'm going with that
I'm a gone daddy, said Mockingbird

Yes you are, said God

Mockingbird Goes to the Suburbs

Mockingbird sang for a while
Then he said, I think I'll eat a bug

And started looking around
Mockingbird got a big idea

And flew out to the suburbs
Every now and then a bird's

Gotta dig a worm, said Mockingbird

Mockingbird and the Working Class

The painter hung on his ladder
Like a cricket climbing a tree
Mockingbird saw this
The painter hummed an archaic tune
Mockingbird sang this too
And the bus loading at the corner
And the radio from the school yard
Up the way
And the lady kept coming
To the bay window
To check on the painter's progress
Mockingbird made this his chorus

Bugs and Doves Bursting in Air

Mockingbird hid in the white pine
He fluttered forth and snatched a gnat in midair
He picked at his white walls for mites
Singing all the while never caring what
The world brings
If the world has anything to say
Well, here it is, says Mockingbird

Mockingbird was insatiable
Cranking out churning up and sucking
The ocean of air for tiny wings
Oh! said Mockingbird, will I ever get my fill?

Suddenly there were doves everywhere
Mockingbird fluttered about checking it out
Everywhere lit as far as the eye is slit
Every pole every wire every limb
Cooing on benches kissing on swings
Moaning and mooing like cows with wings
What is this, said Mockingbird, a convention?
The doves are lovesick he saw
Let them coo, he said
Let them croon and swoon
Too soon their morning's passed
But I must last their evening too

Mockingbird mocked the low
Hoo of the doves coo
He heard the hum of a faraway plane
He mocked this and then the cars
And trucks out on the freeway
He mocked the Highway Department
He mocked the Department of Interior

He mocked the Supreme Court
He looked at the Oval Office beneath him
And cracked up mocking himself
Suddenly a piper cub sputtered out
Of a cumulous cloud and Mockingbird
Burst into the Star Spangled Banner
Oh! said Mockingbird holding his gut
Oh, I gotta let up, I gotta quit
Yeah, he said, this is too good

Mockingbird Goes Solo

Mockingbird's tail feathers quivered
Like an antenna they twitched and
Vibrated and turned quick
Like a rudder to the universe
When Mockingbird thought of his mate
They bounced like an erect penis
Poised and pursing itself

Where is my mate? said Mockingbird

He wheeled and his whitewalls
Flashed in the morning light
As he lit a higher limb
He heard the drunk starlings
Stuttering on a wire and
Muttered it back to himself
Nothing they said seemed to know
He flew to a clothesline and up
To a lamppost then down
To a hood ornament
And over to a mailbox
He stuck his head in a crepe myrtle
Then walked straight down the street
Before flying up to a tree
Then a wire

Where is my mate? said Mockingbird

He hopped atop a telephone pole
Like a crucifix and said nothing

Mockingbird and His Mate

Mockingbird and his mate made
Mad loops in the air flashing their
Two-toned wings like silver fish
Super-imposed on a Technicolor sea
Dive bomber barracuda heat seeking
Missiles out of their everlovin' minds
Bluejay had worms to grub
And eggs to snatch
But he held back
Until they come to their senses
He said, and settle into song
Blackbird needed to get
To the drainage ditch
She had chicks to feed
But as long as Mockingbird
And his shadow zipped and
Zoomed their sudden monsoon
Of loops and dips and dashes
Trashing the air and everyone's
Space with their insane come
Fuck me chase, she would wait

Crow was two blocks away
Crouched over a craning chimney
It was all very fascinating
And sickening to him
He would stop the whole show
If he only knew how
Across the street a dog lay
At the edge of the porch
Pulling back one ear in mystification
Recalling a blinding peck to the top
Of his head

Yes! Sang the Maestro

The mimosa was in full molly bloom
Where Mockingbird danced on a stiff branch
The musk laden flowers heavy
With fellatio in budding crescendo
Mockingbird gulped it in and spewed it out
The landscape lay before him
Like a lady with her legs apart
Yes! sang the maestro opening her lips
Letting his beak speak to parts unknown
Again and again he summoned
His glee pouring forth an effusion
Of symphonic frivolity
The exotic pink flora curling round
His thrilling trilling melody

Mockingbird and the Man

All through the night Mockingbird sang
Waking up the Man again and again
The Man stood at his bedroom window
And listened to Mockingbird
I have no idea
What you are saying, said the Man
I have no idea
What you are saying, said Mockingbird

Next day from a blossoming redbud tree
Mockingbird observed the Man cuddling
His baby on the back porch swing
Ahhyaya wahga doodoowee, said the baby
Ahma gwawa ooowah puhpuh
This made Mockingbird want to sing
But he held his beak
What's that, said the Man
What you trying to tell your papa?
Do you want to tell your papa something?
Some day you'll tell me, said the Man
Yes you will, he laughed, yes you will

Mockingbird went ahead and told him

The Man and the Moth

The Man heard the tiny flap
And tap at the glass before he
Knew what he was knowing
He went to the window
And parted the curtains
Nothing but sunshine
Through a clear glass day
And then the sudden flutter
Coming up from nowhere
And bouncing off the glass
Ascending to the high edge
Of the illusion Moth
Found himself in a prison
The Man watched at the window
Observing closely the intricate
Patterns of Moth's wings when
He stopped to rest sometimes
Walking a ways in determined
Bewilderment before striking
Out again full throttle to rise
Treading air to nowhere
The Man had dropped the
Occupation of his former
Attention and was fully given
Over to the plight of this
Exotic helpless creature
He moved to touch it
But found he was as lost
And shy as what he would
Capture and couldn't imagine
Intruding his fingers into that
Frantic but exquisite flutter
And would just the pressure

Of holding still those precious
Wings harm them in some way
Not worth the effort to free?
Then something in him beyond
His manner and control now
Pulled a switch and triggered
Him forward with great haste
And snagged soft fuzzy Moth
He held him only so well as
To still the wings and transport
Him away from the glass and
Down to the windowpane where
His other hand pushed aloft
The screen just long enough to
Release Moth from his delicate
Grasp with a light spring and
Propulsion and Moth was amazed
As his wings found air and
His motion flew him away
From his former captor into
The free range blue yonder
Amazed as well was Mockingbird
Who watched it all with keen
Interest from the opposite loft
The whole capture and release
And uncertain take off of
Dear Moth who Mockingbird
Swiftly swooped down and
Deftly snatched in mid-flight
And swallowed whole after
Landing back on his perch
Where with a courteous and courtly
Bow he thanked the Man who
Stood at the closed window
With his open mouth

Dance of the Stink Bug

The day began with stink bugs
Arriving on screen doors and windshields
Orbiting in from thin air through open
Windows and garage doors where
Momma pulled laundry from the dryer
As they soundlessly plopped on the clean
Towels looking out like nothing unusual
Starting their little bug-legged dance
Up the palm tree on dude's shirt
Then over to Momma's panties
It was more than you can swallow
And soon enough she took the laundry
Outside and shook them off in the grass
And coming back in closed the garage
Door then the kitchen door behind her
And washed her hands at the window sink
Mockingbird watched it all
From the Japanese maple just
A flutter away in the yard
He was quite amused
He loves this day
The day of the dance of the stink bug
Oh yes, said Mockingbird
Dance little stink bug dance
And let my work begin

The Fall

A funny thing happened to Mockingbird
He fell down a chimney hole
What's so funny about that, said Mockingbird
I'm no Santa Claus
Well, maybe you are?
This looks bad, said Mockingbird
Graceful beyond all reason, he reasoned
And then this happens

Mockingbird was chasing a moth
Dancing around the chimney stack
Of an old Edwardian roof
He made a maneuver that landed
The bug in his beak
But sent him into a black hole
And down he went
No room to spread his wings
Helpless to alter a thing
He hit bottom in another world
A world he'd never seen

Mockingbird sat stunned as
The day he was born
He choked down the moth
With soot on his beak
Dizzy and disheveled he
Tried to focus
And fright upon fright
There stood the Man
Looking back at him
Mockingbird froze
His heart a great flutter
He rose but his motor

Stuttered in the quick
Hands of the Man who
Lifted him up and away
Mockingbird gave a wee
Twerp but felt
Discretion the better
Part of this valor
As he took a ride
Around a corner
Through a hall
Then down some stairs
And suddenly outdoors
In full view of the
World he knew
There, said the Man
There you go
As he placed him
On the ground
And stood back

Well, said Mockingbird
Stretching his feathers
Good to check out your nest
Quite impressive, yes
I'll be moseying along now, he said
And elevated his bad self
To the nearest tree
And then another
And then another
Where he glanced back
The Man still standing
In the doorway

Adieu, said Mockingbird
But he didn't move

The sun slid out of her summer dress
What say we just forget this
Said Mockingbird
And let it go, I would suggest
The Man was watching
The sun slipped out of its gown
Mockingbird flew to another tree
The Man's eyes followed him
My eyesight is a hundred times
Better than yours, said Mockingbird
But still the Man saw through him
Yes, said Mockingbird, yes
Hubris
Before the fall, he sighed
And ventured to a higher limb
Okay, let's not pretend
Let's just say, I was on a mission
And I guess I was, Mockingbird laughed
The Man was still looking
The sun slid into a nice hot bath
Well, it's not easy being
Mockingbird, said Mockingbird
And that was that

Adios, he said, and flew to
The top of the chimney and
Opened his dusty beak
And began to rewrite history

Mockingbird and the Beasts

Dogs were barking all down
The street as UPS found an address
And backed their big brown truck
Up a gravel driveway
Something about words on
Vehicles, thought Mockingbird
Really snaps these mutts to a pitch
The driver got out
Slid the back door open
The little terrier twins ran yapping
To the link fence like firecrackers
Popping off in their bodies
The Doberman next door kept
A snarling pace and tortured path
At the end of his chain
The driver pulled a dolly from
The truck and wheeled three boxes
To the front door where a lady
Came cradling to her bosom
A Siamese cat who gaped none
Too sure of the brown intruder
And shocking cacophony of
Canines that continued unabated
The driver appeared a minute
Later with a ledger and the lady
Set the Siamese down to sign
Her name extending a leg to
Keep the cat from the door
Then the driver loaded the dolly
And pulled the truck back out
And up the road and around
The block and over the hill
With a blistering chorus of howls

Trailing after him until one
By one the dogs ceased their
Barking and stood stunned
Their mouths the shape
Of smoking guns
Eyes cocked wide waiting
For another pulse
From the great brown beast

Mockingbird saw it all from
The eve across the street
He swung down and sat atop the
Barbs of the chain linked fence
He sang a brief but recognizable
Chorus of *Sink the Bismarck*
Before disappearing over the
House through the backyard
And into the neighborhood

Ringing Out the Old

There was a light snow
On the last day of the year
Mockingbird was still there
Marveling at the leftover Christmas
Lights up and down the lane
He'd learned a few new songs
Over the holidays
And sang a little medley
Of these to himself
A week before he'd sat
Inside a Boston fir
Wrapped in sparkly bulbs
And listened to a group
Of carolers gathered round
A silver door
That was pretty good, said Mockingbird
Not bad
They are developing a certain gaiety
In their voices, he thought
A certain joy
In mocking themselves
Mockingbird considered this
He considered the possibility
That someday people might
Come to mock him

The Song of the Spheres

Mockingbird saw the sun disappearing
Behind a wall of wisteria
Slowly closing its eye
Falling away
Sinking down
Into the deep dark sea
Of sleep
See you later, said Mockingbird
And to the east behind a line of trees
He spied the winking moon rising
To his vesper tune
I greet you too, sang Mockingbird
Whose melody arrives on
Far tracks of time
I am the voice of the world, sang Mockingbird
I wave and watch you go by
I sing to your rise and fall
I sing the song that is the world, sang Mockingbird
More than the whale
More than the porpoise
More than the meadowlark and thrush
More than that false prophet rooster
More than man
More than woman
I am the beak of sound, he sang
I am the speak of now

My eye sees the sun
And the sun sees my eye, said Mockingbird
Nothing is lost in the turning, he ariated
I paint an eyeball on chaos, that's all, he chimed
Do I know the sun? said Mockingbird
Do I know the moon?

Do I know the song of the spheres?
I'll show you some spheres, said Mockingbird
And he rolled out the stars like sparkling marbles
Across the darkening sky

Mockingbird and Raven

Come with me, said little Sparrow
Mockingbird wasn't even sure

If she was talking to him
But flew behind the highway sign

Into a junkyard of old cars
Sparrow was nowhere to be seen

But Bluejay nodded and pointed a path
Between the trees that Mockingbird

Followed over a sea of wrecks and
Shacks and junk and dogs on chains

And dogs that weren't and swallows
Swung down on either side lifting him

Along in their breeze and he slid through
A corridor of careless wires and dusty

Leaves to exactly where he wasn't sure
But suddenly he was there surrounded

By pigeons and starlings all living in
Holes under a dilapidated roof ripped

Open at one end where a swath of light
Caved through the dust into the dark

And there perched upon an old tobacco
Pole like some king rooster was the biggest

Blackest Raven he had ever seen
Red eyes smoldering in the

Shadows looking straight through
Mockingbird who instantly flashed

On a thousand lifetimes in less
Than a second

What is this? said Mockingbird
Just take it easy, said Raven

What's going on? said he who
Wanted to know

I just want to chat, said the dark one
His eyes rolling over Mockingbird

Chat? said Mockingbird, chit chat?
Shit on that, he said

Just a word, said Raven
Bird is the word, said Mockingbird

Yes, said Raven, Bird is the word
He leaned slightly forward

Revealing his full ancient head
Bird is the World, he added

Mockingbird heard and wondered
What is this sly Devil up to?

Bird was here before, said Raven
And Bird will be here after

Been doing some long range speculating?
Asked Mockingbird

Yeah, said Raven, Why not?
Why? said Mockingbird

We all got to live together, said Raven
Since when? said Mockingbird

Look, said Raven, I'm making an effort here
And what happens when a thief makes an effort?

Said Mockingbird
Look who's calling who a thief, said Raven

No one even knows who's who or
What's what any more, thanks to you, he said

No one ever knew squat, said Mockingbird
No one ever knew what 's what

Except that what you got in your talons
Wasn't yours, said Mockingbird

Except that what you got in your beak
Wasn't yours, said Raven

And what I've got in my talons
Is very much mine, he quickly added

And what I've got in my beak
Is all mine, said Mockingbird

He felt the starlings hover at their holes
The pigeons turned to clay

Okay, said Mockingbird, did you have
Me here just to play that broken record?

I have you here, said Raven, hoping
We can move forward

Where you going, asked Mockingbird
Any place I know?

Yeah, said Raven, we're going round
And round the sun, just like you

Is this your news? said Mockingbird
Look, said Raven, can't we just show

A little consideration for a mighty tribe
Your formidable and distinguished foe?

A gang of thieves, thought Mockingbird
But he only raised his wings and stretched

His feathers and let Raven's words
Settle in the choked air

Consideration, what does that look like
To you? asked Mockingbird

That looks like a day in the park without
Some bully beatin' up on the young ones

Said Raven, like a little shopping spree
Without having to encounter our damnation

From a street preacher at every corner
We all have our work, said Mockingbird

Yes, we all have our work, said Raven
And we'll try to leave you to it

Sounds reasonable, said Mockingbird
Believing not a word of it

Let's just see how it goes, offered Raven
Let's just see how it goes, mocked Mocker

And go he did through the hole in the roof
And straight into the future

The Crack Between The Worlds

Mockingbird was having his quiet time
While the jar flies banged their brains
Against the twilight gloss
Mockingbird found the damp spots
In the side yard where daddy's
After dinner hose left puddles
And dug worms with ease

There's a lot to think about
Thought Mockingbird
But you can think too much
He thought again
It is enough to know I am the river
I am the puddle, he said, I am the sea
I am a pretty blue melody floating
Among stars sailing through swirls
And whirls of light
I'm holding up this end, said Mockingbird
Yes I am

When Mockingbird had his fill
He rested his mind
He thought of all the eggs that came
Before him and all the eggs to come
Let go your thoughts, he thought
Let go your thoughts
And all his thoughts dropped
They dropped through the dark sea
At the bottom of the world
And there he sank
Like a crow through a black hole
Like the silence of the sun
He sank through the crack

Between the worlds
Disappearing
Down

And

Down

And

When he looked again
There was only darkness
And darkness said nothing
Okay, said Mockingbird
And lifted himself up
To a tattered wire
And sang his heart out

Mockingbird and the Broken Wheel of the Sky

Mockingbird was his own microphone
      his own cell phone
      his own hollow bone
He was his own news reporter
      his own sports announcer
      his own counselor
      his own muse
Mockingbird was his own observatory
      his own depository
      his own museum of science and history
      his own way in
      his own way out
He was his own mirror
      his own echo
      his own city
      his own omen
      his own prophecy

Mockingbird was the eminent and immaculate artiste
He was a swirl in the spherical curl of the world
A salutation to life in all its verities, vagaries, and vicissitudes
A vanity to the mud-caked breath of existence itself

Mockingbird held in his beak the cracked shell OM
Of the moon-tweaked sea at dawn
Passing through his breath was the lilted lip of clouds
Coming through the mountain pass
Mockingbird firmly grasped in his beak
The unspeakable creaking axle of the galaxy
The brown and broken worm of Time

And Mockingbird Sang

It was a beautiful lost summer day
Everything was full of itself
And nothing more than Mockingbird
And not a soul knew why or what
Had wrought its creation or cared
To think and no one less
Than Mockingbird
He played with the wind
He played with the chimes
He was the wind and chimes
And when the sun had reached its zenith
Mockingbird sang out
Echoing a grove of willows
God's own horn tuning the sky
Let's get this going, said God
Let's get this going, said Mockingbird
And every bird that heard
Was heard to sing
Wonder
Wonder
Wonder
A chorus of wonder
And the trees chimed in
What whirl it is
What whirl it is
And all the grasses played golden harps
OOooOO OMMMM
Amen, said Mockingbird
Let's begin, said Mockingbird
World without end, said Mockingbird
World without end!

R.B. Morris is a poet and songwriter, solo performer and band leader, and sometimes playwright and actor. He has published books of poetry, including EARLY FIRES (Iris Press) and KEEPING THE BEES EMPLOYED (Rich Mountain Bound), and music albums including SPIES LIES AND BURNING EYES and his most recent solo project RICH MOUNTAIN BOUND. He wrote and acted in THE MAN WHO LIVES HERE IS LOONY, a one-man play taken from the life and work of James Agee, and was instrumental in founding a park dedicated to Agee in Knoxville. Morris served as the Jack E. Reese Writer-in-Residence at the University of Tennessee from 2004-2008, and was inducted into the East Tennessee Writers Hall of Fame in 2009. He lives in Knoxville.

www.rbmorris.com

CPSIA information can be obtained
at www.ICGtesting.com
Printed in the USA
LVOW11s0558100817
544492LV00001B/18/P